Corythosaurus

Written by Frances Swann
Illustrated by Pam Mara

Library of Congress Cataloging-in-Publication Data

Swann, Frances 1955–
  Corythosaurus.

  (Dinosaur library)
  Summary: Follows a Corythosaurus through a typical day as she feeds, prepares to lay her eggs, and interacts with other dinosaurs.
  1. Corythosaurus – Juvenile literature.
[1. Corythosaurus.   2. Dinosaurs]   I. Title.   II. Series.
QE862.065S93   1988   567.9'7   87-36915
ISBN 0-86592-521-6

Rourke Enterprises, Inc.
Vero Beach, FL 32964

Quetzalcoatlus

Parasaurolphus

Deinosuchus

Corythasaurus

Spinosaurus

Oviraptor

Corythosaurus

Pachycephalosaurus

Anatosaurus

Struthiomimus

Scolosaurus

Rutiodon

Psittacosaurus

Dusk was falling over the great oak forest as the Corythosaurus herd began to settle for the night. Gradually the familiar sounds of the day faded, and the warm air was filled with the rustling noises of the night.

A little way from the herd, a pair of Stenonychosaurus hunted their evening meal of small mammals. The Corythosaurus watched the Stenonychosaurus lazily as they darted over the forest floor, their large eyes missing nothing. Satisified, the two Stenonychosaurus departed, and in the fading light, Corythosaurus and her herd fell asleep.

Corythosaurus awoke to the familiar smells of the forest on a spring day. She felt hungry. The herd gradually gathered together and moved off. Walking slowly on all fours, they headed toward the river. Corythosaurus, the other females, and the youngsters stayed in the center of the herd. The males, ever watchful, surrounded them.

When they arrived at a cypress grove, the herd spread out to feed. Standing on her back legs, Corythosaurus reached up and broke off twigs with her jaws. As she chewed she watched last year's youngsters forage in the undergrowth. She felt content. The forest was peaceful. Over the last few weeks the sounds of the males' noisy mating displays had filled the air. Soon Corythosaurus would return to the nest site to lay her eggs in the sand.

Well fed, the herd re-grouped and moved on. The undergrowth was thicker now. The canopy of poplar and willow leaves above them let in more light, and Corythosaurus could feel the sun on her back.

Suddenly aware of movement, the herd stopped and stared in astonishment. There before them was a pair of male Chasmosaurus. Both were nodding their great frilled heads violently from side to side in a mating display. Then, apparently unaware of the herd's presence, they charged each other, locking their browhorns together.

The herd was startled into action by the noise and moved quickly away toward swampier ground.

The air was hot and humid, and the smell of rotting vegetation and stagnant water hung in the air. Corythosaurus nibbled from the china firs as she walked. Beneath her feet the wet ground was littered with fallen moss—covered branches. Every so often a heron flapped lazily away as she approached.

A Struthiomimus appeared. Agile and alert, it ran backwards and forwards hunting the dragonflies that skimmed the pools. Corythosaurus watched it with curiosity. Soon it caught a frog with a loud snap, swallowed it, and ran off toward the forest.

A sudden commotion at the edge of the forest brought the herd to an abrupt halt. In the split second before she fled, Corythosaurus saw a lone Centrosaurus cornered by an Albertosaurus; its huge frame towered over its prey. As the Centrosaurus charged, the Albertosaurus wavered and then turned away.

Terrified, Corythosaurus and her herd raced for the safety of the river. On reaching the water, they splashed out through the shallows until they could swim. Only when they knew the water was too deep for the Albertosaurus to reach them did they begin to relax.

The river was wide and winding. The herd swam upstream, keeping a careful distance between them and the shore. Corythosaurus felt exhausted. The sun reflected on the water and dazzled her eyes. Still the herd swam on. Above them Corythosaurus could see several Pteranodon soaring on the warm air currents, probably heading for the sea.

The herd was now quite far away from Albertosaurus. Corythosaurus felt safer and followed the others into the shallows, where they waded quietly in the warm water.

Rested, they moved back towards the swamp. A large herd of Parasaurolophus passed close by. The herds ignored one another, each knowing the other posed no threat.

Corythosaurus and the others fed as they skirted the edge of the forest. The light was fading slowly, and all seemed peaceful.

A strange distant noise stopped the herd. Corythosaurus stood alert. She scented the air, sensing danger. Suddenly over the heads of the leading males she could see the cause. On the other side of the swamp two huge Tyrannosaurs and an Albertosaurus were scavenging a dinosaur carcass. At their feet a pair of large crocodiles fought over the remains.

Intent on their meal, the Tyrannosaurus appeared not to have noticed the herd. Once again the herd turned and fled. This time they ran headlong into the forest.

Only when they reached the protective darkness of the oak forest did they stop. Corythosaurus stood wearily, her flanks heaving. The herd would go no farther tonight. Corythosaurus found a soft part of the forest floor and lay down. Night was falling, and the day had been eventful. She was ready to sleep.

Corythosaurus and the Cretaceous World

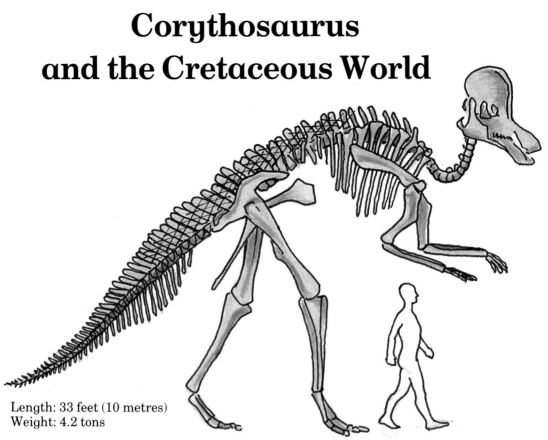

Length: 33 feet (10 metres)
Weight: 4.2 tons

The skeleton of Corythosaurus compared in size with a man.

The Age of the Dinosaurs

The word dinosaur is derived from two Greek words meaning "terrible lizard". All the dinosaur lived in the Mesozoic era, 225 to 64 million years ago, at a time when the continents were much closer to one another than they are today. At one time much of the land was one giant continent called Pangea. This great land mass broke up over many millions of years, and segments drifted apart to become the continents as we know them today.

No human being has ever seen a dinosaur. Human beings did not appear on earth until 2 to 3 million years ago. How do we know so much about the dinosaurs?

Fossil finds

Our knowledge comes from fossils that have been discovered all over the world. Scientists have found fossil skeletons, eggs, nesting sites, tracks, dung, imprints of skin, and even mummified stomach contents. Every day new finds tell us more about the dinosaurs and their world.

When Corythosaurus Lived

The Mesozoic Age is divided into three eras: Triassic, Jurassic, and Cretaceous. Corythosaurus lived at the end of the Cretaceous era, which lasted from 135 to 64 million years ago. The word Cretaceous means chalk. During this time great beds of chalk were laid down, and the continents took on their current shapes. At the beginning of the Cretaceous era the weather was mild, but by the end it had become much colder.

The sea levels were high, and the land was low-lying, with many deltas, rivers, lakes and swamps. Many new kinds of plants evolved during the Cretaceous era. Flowering plants appeared for the first time. By the end of the Cretaceous period many trees and plants existed that would be familiar to us today .

All About Corythosaurus

Fossil remains of Corythosaurus have been found in South America, Asia, Europe, and North America. Corythosaurus was a Hadrosaurid dinosaur, often called a "Duckbill".

Corythosaurus was a medium-sized dinosaur which could walk on either two or four feet. Her paddle-like hands and strong deep tail show that she could certainly swim. This ability to swim was her main defense against predators.

Corythosaurus had a sharp, horny, tortoise-like beak. Fossilized stomach remains show that hadrosaurids fed on conifer needles, twigs, land plants and seeds. Corythosaurus had hundreds of large grinding teeth; some hadrosaurids had over a thousand teeth.

The word Corythosaurus means "helmet lizard." A male Corythosaurus had a larger crest than the females and the young. It is thought that displaying males used their crests as a signal. They also signaled by making noises.

Corythosaurus would have laid eggs and probably used the same site each year to nest and care for her young.

Other Dinosaurs in this Book
Stenonychosaurus

A 6 foot, 6-inch (2 meters) dinosaur from Canada. Stenonychosaurus is thought to have been one of the most intelligent of the dinosaurs. Its big round eyes may have helped it hunt its prey in bad light.

Chamosaurus

A 17 foot (5.2 meters) dinosaur from New Mexico, and Alberta, Canada. Chamosaurus had a huge frill around its neck. Big skin-covered "holes" in the frill reduced its weight.

Struthiomimus

A 10 to 13 foot dinosaur from New Jersey and Alberta, Canada. Struthiomimus was an "ostrich dinosaur." It fed on fruits, seeds, insects, and small creatures. Struthiomimus would have been able to outrun its predators.

Albertosaurus

A 26 foot (8 meters) dinosaur from Montana and Alberta, Canada. Albertosaurus was a tryrannosaurid dinosaur – a flesh eating group. They had small front limbs, muscular limbs, and short deep jaws with large sharp teeth.

Tyrannosaurus

A 39 foot long (12 meters) dinosaur from North America. Tyrannosaurus was about 18 feet 6 inches (5.6 meters) high and weighed about 7 tons. Tyrannosaurus was massive, the biggest flesh-eating dinosaur. Tyrannosaurus may have lived mainly by eating dead animals; its huge size probably made hunting difficult.

Centrosaurus

A 20 foot (6 meters) dinosaur from Alberta, Canada. Centrosaurus had a single nose-horn, spines, horns on its neck frill, and hooves like a rhino. Centrosaurus was built to be very powerful. It would probably charge if attacked.

Parasaurolophus

A 33 foot (10 meters) dinosaur from Utah, New Mexico, and Alberta, Canada. Parasaurolophus belonged to the same hadrosaurid group of dinosaurs as Corythosaurus. Their lifestyles would have been very similar. Parasaurolophus had a hollow horn 6 feet (1.8 meters) long that curved back over its head. Air in the hollow horn probably produced a loud, distinctive trumpeting call.

Pteranodon

Pteranodon was not a dinosaur but a flying reptile, a pterosaur. One kind of pterosaur, called Quezalcoatlus, had a 50 foot (15 meter) wing span. This is the same size as a small light aircraft.